CONTENTS

DEEP SPACE: THE NEXT FRONTIER

The ISS **orbits** more than 320 kilometres (200 miles) above Earth. This distance is considered Low Earth Orbit (LEO). LEO is between 159 and 1,931 km (99 and 1,200 miles) above Earth's surface. Many space missions have been within this distance.

Deep space goes beyond LEO. Sometimes called outer space, deep space is outside the pull of Earth's **gravity**. Deep space includes the Moon and planets in our **solar system**. Scientists are designing more space missions to go further than we've gone before.

orbit travel around an object in space

gravity force that pulls objects together; gravity pulls objects down towards the centre of Earth

solar system the Sun and all the planets, moons, comets and smaller bodies orbiting it

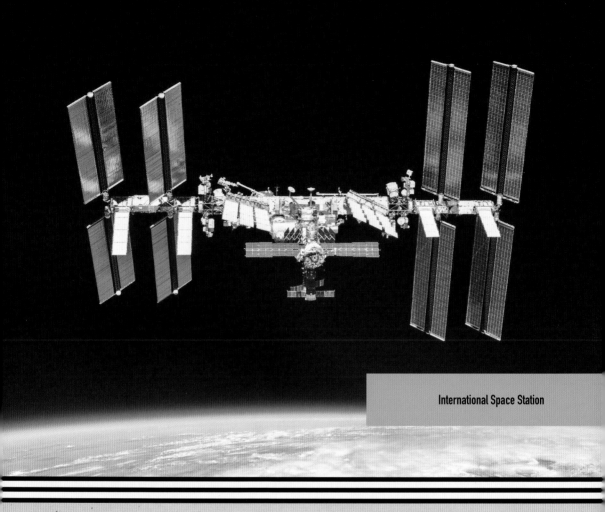

Gravity

Throw a ball up in the air. No matter how hard you throw it, the ball will always fall to the ground. This happens because of gravity. Gravity pulls objects towards the centre of Earth. It keeps objects – and humans – from floating away into space.

To get a spacecraft into outer space, it has to escape Earth's gravity. To do that, it needs a large and powerful rocket.

CHAPTER TWO

ORION AND THE SLS

NASA, along with more than 1,000 **aerospace**, technology and engineering companies, is building a rocket system to get spacecraft into deep space. The Space Launch System (SLS) will be the most advanced rocket system ever built. It's made to go further into space than any rocket has gone before. The SLS is scheduled to launch in 2020. Scientists believe the SLS is the answer to getting humans into deep space.

But the SLS is only part of the solution. To explore new worlds in space, astronauts need a spacecraft. NASA and the European Space Agency (ESA) have built a spacecraft for the job. It's called the Orion Multi-Purpose Crew Vehicle.

SPACE FACT

NASA stands for the National Aeronautics and Space Administration.

A rocket launched Orion into space on 5 December 2014.

Before any spacecraft can carry astronauts into space, it must be tested first. Orion's first test was in 2014. NASA sent Orion into Earth's orbit without astronauts on board. It was launched on a Delta IV rocket. Orion travelled at a speed of 32,000 km (20,000 miles) per hour. Then it safely returned to Earth. The test flight was a success.

aerospace science and technology of jet flight and space travel

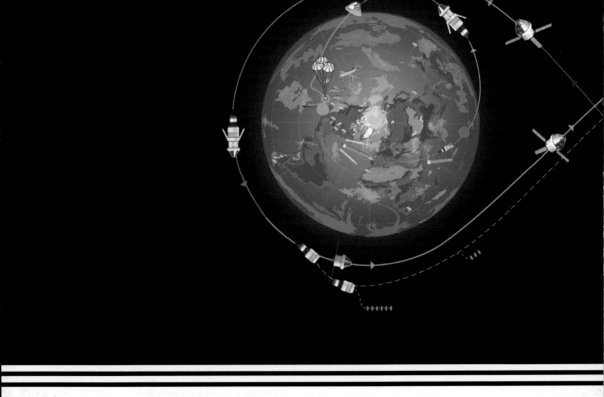

In 2020 scientists plan to test Orion again.
This mission is called Exploration Mission-1
(EM-1). Orion will sit on top of the SLS, 98 metres
(321 feet) above the launch pad. That's about the
height of Big Ben! Together, Orion and SLS will weigh
more than 2.3 million kilograms (5 million pounds).
The SLS will push Orion away from Earth at a speed
up to 39,400 km (24,500 miles) per hour.

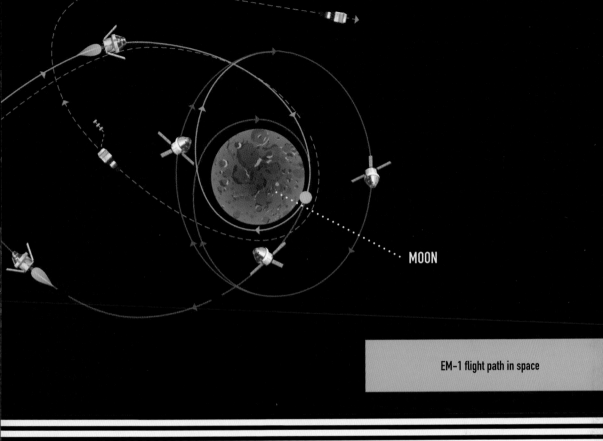

MOON

Once in space, Orion will separate from the SLS. Then it will travel 2.1 million km (1.3 million miles) around the Moon and back to Earth. No astronauts will be on board this mission. Scientists need to make sure the rocket and spacecraft work as planned before adding astronauts.

Part of the Orion spacecraft

SPACE FACT

Orion's journey around the Moon will take between eight days and three weeks.

If Orion's EM-1 is a success, Orion's next mission will travel the same path. Exploration Mission-2 (EM-2) is scheduled for 2023. This time, four astronauts will be on board. If the mission is successful, scientists hope Orion will take astronauts to Mars or even further into space.

People behind the astronauts

Astronauts are an important part of any successful space mission. But hundreds of people work on the ground providing support to the astronauts. These workers include scientists, engineers, technicians, designers, pilots and radio operators. Some gather data from spacecraft and launch facilities. Others analyse data and make decisions based on their findings.

If problems arise in space, there's little time to make critical decisions. This is why engineers and scientists do **simulations** with astronauts. They work together to find solutions to issues. That way, they can be ready if the same issues happen in space.

simulation act of imitating what will or could happen in real life

CHAPTER THREE

LIVING IN SPACE

What will astronauts need to survive in deep space? Humans need air, food and water to live. Astronauts also need space to move, especially during long missions. And the spacecraft needs to be kept at the correct temperature.

When designing Orion, NASA and ESA kept all of this in mind. Astronauts will be seated in the Orion crew **module** during lift-off. This area will also be a living space during their mission.

module separate section that can be linked to other parts

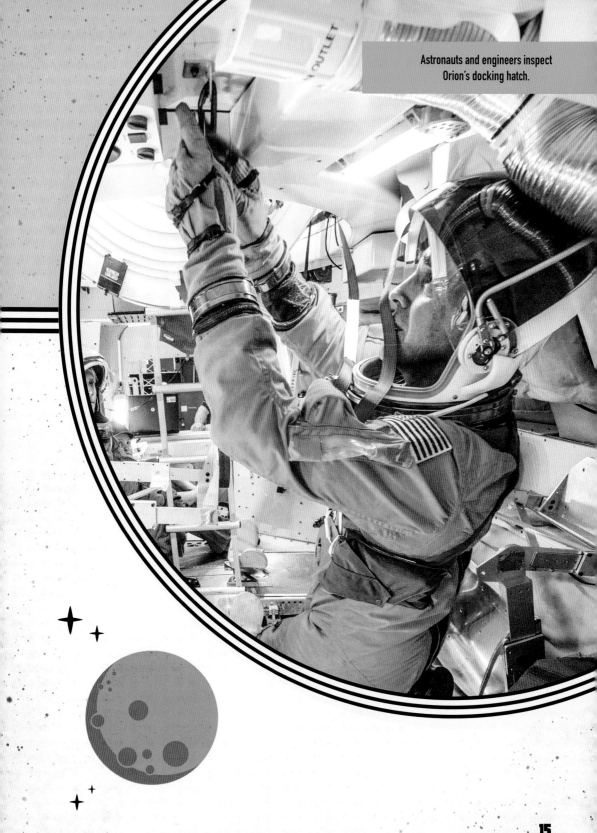

Astronauts and engineers inspect Orion's docking hatch.

Orion's crew module can fit up to six astronauts on board. It will be about 5 metres (16 feet) wide and 3 m (10 feet) high. No matter how hot or cold space is outside, the module will stay at 22 degrees Celsius (72 degrees Fahrenheit). Astronauts won't have a lot of room, but scientists will try to make them as comfortable as possible.

A view of what the inside of Orion's crew module will look like

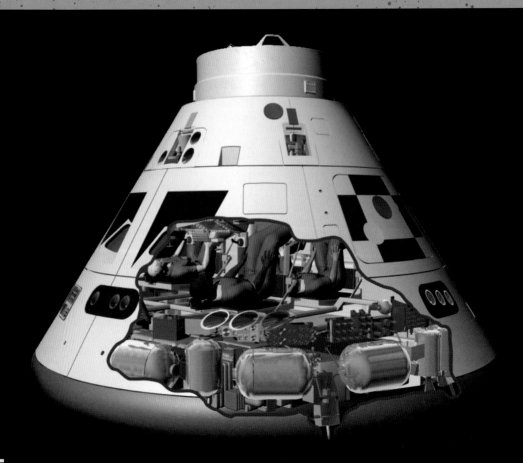

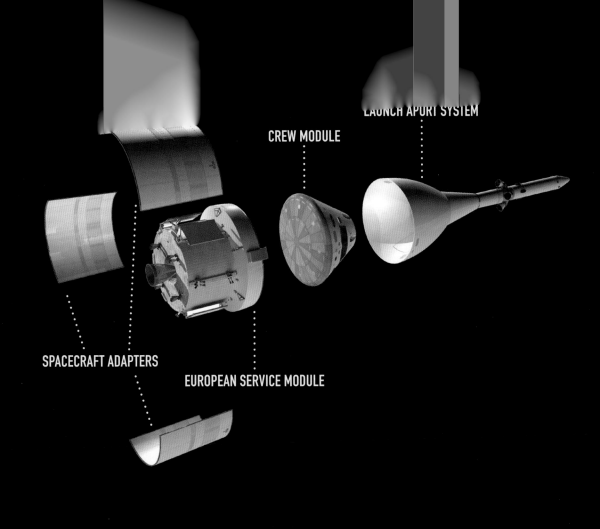

CREW MODULE

LAUNCH ABORT SYSTEM

SPACECRAFT ADAPTERS

EUROPEAN SERVICE MODULE

A 2015 digital drawing of Orion

As space missions last longer, astronauts
will need more room to move inside. Scientists will
base new designs on how astronauts live on the ISS.

ESA built the service module for Orion. This part provides the spacecraft's water, air and electricity. The service module also holds tanks of fuel for Orion's engines. The module will have **solar panels**. The panels will gather energy from the Sun to provide electricity for the spacecraft. Three panels make up a solar array wing. Each wing is 6.7 metres (22 feet) long. The spacecraft has four solar array wings. When Orion is in darkness, rechargeable batteries will store power until the solar panels can be used again.

At the end of Orion's mission, the service module will fall away. Only the crew module carrying the astronauts will return to Earth. Any high-speed object travelling through the **atmosphere** must withstand temperatures as high as 2,760 degrees C (5,000 degrees F). To keep astronauts safe as Orion speeds back towards Earth, scientists created a heat shield. It's the largest heat shield in the world and is located at the base of the crew module. The shield will focus the heat away from the astronauts inside. Once Orion gets through the atmosphere, strong parachutes will help it land safely in the sea. Then US Navy ships will pick up the astronauts.

solar panel flat surface that collects sunlight and turns it into power
atmosphere layer of gases that surrounds some planets, dwarf planets and moons

Solar panels will collect the Sun's energy
to make electricity for Orion.

CHAPTER FOUR

NEXT STOP, MARS

One of NASA's space exploration plans is called Moon to Mars. The Moon is much closer to Earth than Mars. This makes it an ideal place to develop new technology and systems for deep space. What we build and learn on the Moon can be used on future missions to Mars.

Many countries are planning missions to the Moon. China and the European Space Agency (ESA) hope to build a habitat there called a moon village. This permanent village is seen as the first step to reaching and exploring Mars. China and ESA hope to build the village by 2030. India also plans to send astronauts to the Moon. Several space agencies, including NASA and ESA, are working together on a lunar space station called the Lunar Orbital Platform-Gateway.

The Lunar Orbital Platform-Gateway will be the first crewed space station near the Moon. Scientists want it to include a small habitat for the crew, communications station, science lab and docking station for visiting spacecraft. The Gateway would test long-term missions in deep-space environments.

One day the Aurora Station will be able to hold six guests in space.

Aurora Station

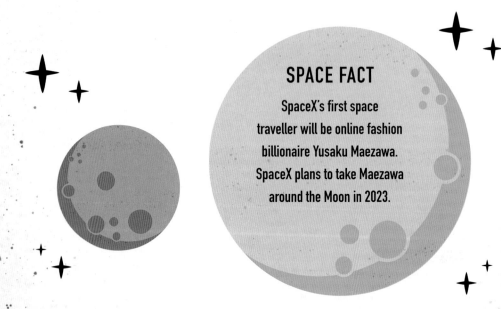

SPACE FACT

SpaceX's first space traveller will be online fashion billionaire Yusaku Maezawa. SpaceX plans to take Maezawa around the Moon in 2023.

SPACE TOURISM

Imagine if you could go to the Moon on holiday or take a ride around Earth in a spacecraft. This may be possible sooner than you think. Private companies such as SpaceX, Virgin Galactic and Blue Origin are planning such missions. Tickets will cost between £150,000 and £240,000. The first flights will be to suborbital space, about 100 km (62 miles) above Earth. But someday people could take one- to two-week holidays on space stations orbiting Earth!

CHAPTER FIVE

THE RED PLANET

NASA's Moon to Mars Exploration mission is just one of many exploration plans. Private companies and countries such as China are also interested in sending humans to Mars.

At present, unmanned **probes** are up on Mars. Scientists use them to study different parts of the planet. Scientists are also learning about the atmosphere, land and climate of Mars. The latest probe to land on the red planet was NASA's InSight. It landed near Mars's equator on 26 November 2018. InSight's mission will last at least two years.

probe small, unmanned spacecraft sent to gather data

InSight took this photo of itself in December 2018.

Two tiny **satellites** followed InSight to its destination on Mars. Known as Mars Cube One (MarCO), these satellites served as a relay system for InSight to communicate with Earth during its landing.

Further than we imagined

In 1977 NASA launched two probes into space. Voyager 1 and Voyager 2 took photos of Jupiter, Saturn, Uranus and Neptune. When their mission was over, the probes kept going deeper into space. They continue to collect data today.

The Voyager probes have gone further than any human-made object has ever travelled. In 2012 Voyager 1 crossed into **interstellar** space. This part of space is beyond the Sun's magnetic field. Voyager 2 followed in November 2018. The Voyager probes will continue travelling through space until their power runs out.

CubeSats fly above Mars in this digitally created image.

The MarCO satellites are a type of CubeSat. A CubeSat is a small, boxy satellite about the size of a briefcase. The MarCO satellites became the first CubeSats to go beyond Earth's orbit into deep space. They flew within 4,000 km (2,500 miles) of Mars's surface.

interstellar between the stars, most often used to describe travel from one star to another

PROBES AND RADIATION

Sending probes to Mars helps scientists learn about potential dangers to humans, including space **radiation**. The atmosphere and a magnetic field help to shield Earth from the Sun's radiation. There's also radiation in space. Mars doesn't have the same protection.

Today's spacecraft are built to protect astronauts from this radiation. But living on a planet without an Earth-like atmosphere could expose people to high levels of radiation. Data collected from probes could help scientists build better habitats for humans on new planets.

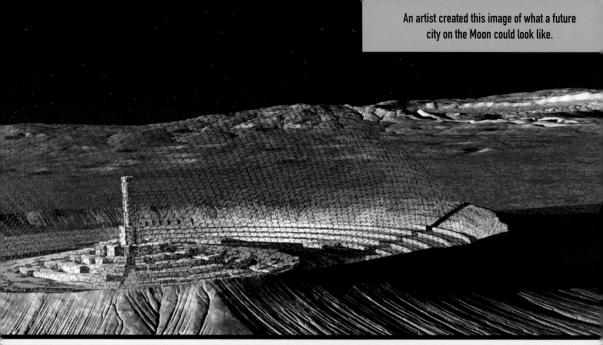

Many exciting developments in space exploration are happening all over the world. As technology advances, so do the opportunities to explore deep space. Perhaps one day scientists will create rockets and spacecraft to take us to distant planets. We may even see people living on the Moon or holidaying on Mars in the near future!

radiation rays of energy given off by certain elements

aerospace science and technology of jet flight and space travel

asteroid chunk of rock that orbits the Sun; asteroids are too small to be called planets

atmosphere layer of gases that surrounds some planets, dwarf planets and moons

engineer someone trained to design and build machines, vehicles, bridges, roads and other structures

gravity force that pulls objects together; gravity pulls objects down towards the centre of Earth

International Space Station place for astronauts to live and work in space

interstellar between the stars, most often used to describe travel from one star to another

module separate section that can be linked to other parts

orbit travel around an object in space

probe small, unmanned spacecraft sent to gather data

radiation rays of energy given off by certain elements

satellite object that moves around a planet or other cosmic body; often a spacecraft used to send signals and information from one place to another

simulation act of imitating what will or could happen in real life

solar panel flat surface that collects sunlight and turns it into power

solar system the Sun and all the planets, moons, comets and smaller bodies

FIND OUT MORE

Fly to Mars! Forces in Space (Feel the Force), Louise and Richard Spilsbury (Raintree, 2015)

Mars Rover Driver (The Coolest Jobs on the Planet), Scott Maxwell & Catherine Chambers (Raintree, 2014)

Mars, The Red Planet: Rocks, Rovers, Pioneers and More! Elizabeth Carney (National Geographic Kids, 2016)

Welcome to Mars: Making a Home on the Red Planet, Buzz Aldrin with Marianne Dyson (National Geographic Kids, 2015)

WEBSITES

DK Find Out facts on Mars
www.dkfindout.com/uk/space/solar-system/mars/

NASA Mars exploration
mars.nasa.gov/participate/funzone/

National Geographic Kids mission to Mars
kids.nationalgeographic.com/explore/space/mission-to-mars/
#mars-planet.jpg

INDEX